TOUCH TYPING IN TEN HOURS

ANN DOBSON

REVISED AND UPDATED THIRD EDITION
How to use the essentials of Microsoft Word 2007

howtobooks

Published by How To Books Ltd,
Spring Hill House, Spring Hill Road,
Begbroke, Oxford OX5 1RX
Tel: (01865) 375794. Fax: (01865) 379162
info@howtobooks.co.uk
www.howtobooks.co.uk

How To Books greatly reduce the carbon footprint of their books by
sourcing their typesetting and printing in the UK

First published 2002
Reprinted 2003
Reprinted 2004
Reprinted 2006
Second edition 2007
Third edition 2009
Reprinted 2009
Reprinted 2011

British Library Cataloguing in Publication Data.
A catalogue record for this book is available from the British Library.

ISBN: 978 1 84528 340 7

Cover design by Baseline Arts Ltd, Oxford
Produced for How To Books by Deer Park Productions, Tavistock
Typeset and design by Baseline Arts Ltd, Oxford
Printed and bound in Great Britain by Bell & Bain Ltd, Glasgow

NOTE: The material contained in this book is set out in good faith for
general guidance and no liability can be accepted for loss or expense
incurred as a result of relying in particular circumstances on statements
made in this book. Laws and regulations are complex and liable to
change, and readers should check the current position with the relevant
authorities before making personal arrangements.

Contents

Part 2 – Additional Touch Typing Practice Material

Part 3 – Microsoft Word Theory

Part 4 – Reference Guide

Illustrations

PREFACE

Almost everyone today has to use a keyboard. Of course it is possible to use two fingers, or even three, and stumble along making lots of mistakes and taking an age to type a single document. But there is a better way. Why not learn to touch type with the help of this new and easy to use book?

Most keyboards still have the traditional QWERTY layout which was first introduced in the days of manual typewriters, so that the most frequently used keys did not 'jam' together. The diagram on each drill page shows this layout and the hand chart shows which finger to use for each key.

As laptops are very popular for an increasingly mobile workforce, I have included a section on using a laptop rather than a traditional keyboard for touch typing.

And new for this Third Edition is a separate section giving simple instructions on how to use Microsoft Word 2007 to produce professional looking documents. All the basics as well as more advanced tasks are included.

Touch typing is easy and fun! That is the message this book seeks to convey. Gone are the days when it took months of laborious learning to master the keyboard. In just ten hours you will be able to type using the right fingers for the right keys. Then gradually, using the additional practice material, your speed will increase, and the reference guide at the back of the book will provide you with all the essential information you need to become proficient in setting out the important business documents of today.

Just think, a few hours now will teach you a skill that will be with you for life. What have you got to lose? Take the book home and start working through it today. By this time next week your hard work will be paying off.

ACKNOWLEDGEMENTS

I would like to thank my daughter Suzannah for her help in updating the book for this Third Edition.

Ann Dobson

INTRODUCTION

Getting Started

Before beginning to touch type you will need suitable equipment. Today this will usually be either a desktop or laptop computer and a word processing package such as Microsoft Word. You will also need a good sized desk and adjustable chair with a supporting backrest.

Correct sitting position

How you position yourself at your desk will determine your comfort whilst touch typing. In particular, take heed of the following:

◆ HEAD. This should be erect. If you tilt your head forwards it puts a strain on your neck. So does watching your fingers. A poor head position can result in headaches.

◆ SHOULDERS. These should be relaxed.

◆ ELBOWS. Keep them close to your body.

◆ FINGERS. Curve your fingers, but not unnaturally so. You may need to raise your fingers more if you are using a laptop computer rather than a traditional keyboard. This is because the keys on a laptop are closer together and the keyboard itself is flatter.

◆ WRISTS. Your wrists should be flat. Aim for a straight line from the knuckles of your middle fingers to your elbows.

◆ FEET. Keep your feet flat on the floor and do not cross your legs.

Specific points for using a laptop computer

Typing on a laptop is not as easy as using a conventional keyboard. You will need to raise your fingers, rather like typing on an old-fashioned manual typewriter, in order to compensate for the keys being closer together and the flatter board. You might find it preferable to plug in an external keyboard whilst you are learning to touch type or to use a cordless keyboard, although if you plan to use your laptop all the time it could be best to learn on it from the beginning.

Most laptops come with a touchpad and at least two buttons underneath it. When you move your fingers over the touchpad it moves the cursor on your screen. The left and right buttons underneath it are similar to the left and right buttons on a mouse. Some laptops also have a centre button which acts as a 4-way scroll, to scroll up or down and move left or right on a page. If you are not happy with this arrangement it is a simple job to plug in an external mouse, or use a cordless mouse.

General points to bear in mind whatever type of computer you use

◆ Use a copy holder whenever possible. They can be purchased cheaply and either stand on the desk or are attached to the monitor. At first it will be best to place the hand chart on this holder, but eventually your work can go there, thus reducing the chance of any eye strain.

◆ Make sure the room lighting is correct. If you are working in an office various rules and regulations will dictate where your equipment is positioned. If you are at home make sure you have the window behind your monitor. There should be no glare, either from lighting or sunshine. It is possible to buy a filter to place on the front of your monitor screen.

◆ Move about frequently so that you don't stiffen up. Take regular breaks – at least ten minutes every hour.

◆ Have regular eye checks – at least every two years.

And off we go . . .

Use the Courier New font, 12 point size for all the drills. (See Reference Guide page 109.) This is what we call a fixed font so that each letter takes up the same amount of space, and your lines will all finish at the same point. It is also a good idea to use double line spacing (see Reference Guide page 108), so that you can see your work more clearly.

There are eight keys on the keyboard known as the 'Home Keys'. They are situated in the middle of the keyboard, and from left to right they are a, s, d, f, j, k, l, ;. The four fingers of your left hand go over the a s d f and the four fingers of your right hand go over the j k l and ;. Most computer keyboards have raised points on the f and j to help you locate the right keys without looking. Your fingers should always hover over these eight keys and from this position you reach up and down to every letter, figure and symbol on the keyboard. (See the hand chart for guidance.)

Type each line until it is perfect and, most importantly, until it can be typed without looking at the keys or your fingers. This is what is known as 'touch typing'. At first each line may take many attempts but this does not matter.

Remember

◆ Keep your fingers on the Home Keys.

◆ Say the letters to yourself as you type them.

◆ Make sure you do not get into bad habits by using the wrong finger for the letter you are typing.

◆ Glance at the hand chart whenever necessary – do not look at the keys or your fingers.

◆ Go slowly – work at your own pace. Speed and accuracy need to come together.

◆ Watch your posture.

Above all, remember that successful touch typing takes time and effort. There is nothing clever about it – determination and hard work singles out the good from the bad – as in most things. If you are tired, something starts to ache or everything starts to go wrong, leave it for another time. You will be surprised just how quickly your speed and accuracy will build up if you work hard enough.

So what are you waiting for?!

LEFT

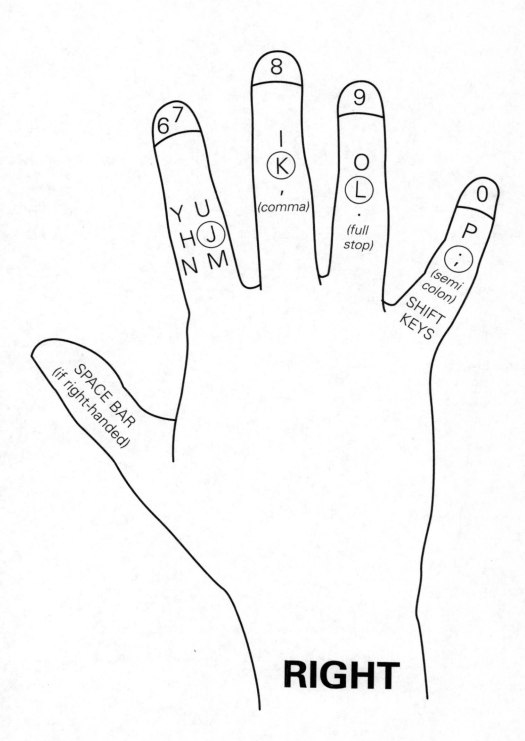

RIGHT

PART 1
DRILLS

HOUR 1: the home keys

The home keys

Remember: Type the line, check, type again if you make a mistake. No delete key to be used.

asdf fdsa asdf fdsa asdf fdsa asdf fdsa asdf fdsa asdf fdsa

jkl; ;lkj jkl; ;lkj jkl; ;lkj jkl; ;lkj jkl; ;lkj jkl; ;lkj

asdf jkl; asdf jkl; asdf jkl; asdf jkl; asdf jkl; asdf jkl;

;lkj fdsa ;lkj fdsa ;lkj fdsa ;lkj fdsa ;lkj fdsa ;lkj fdsa

a s d f j k l ; a s d f j k l ; a s d f j k l ; a s d f j k

; l k j f d s a ; l k j f d s a ; l k j f d s a ; l k j f d

f j d k s l a ; f j d k s l a ; f j d k s l a ; f j d k s l

all; fall falls fad; dad; sad; lad; lass fads dads ask alas

alas ask dads fads lass lad; sad; dad; fad; falls fall all;

dad asks a lad; dad asks a lass; all dads ask alas; ask all

all dads ask; all lads ask; a lass asks; a jaffa asks a lad

Consolidation

Remember: Type the line, check, type again if you make a mistake. No delete key to be used.

asdf jkl; asdf jkl; asdf jkl; asdf jkl; asdf jkl; asdf jkl;

fjdk sla; fjdk sla; fjdk sla; fjdk sla; fjdk sla; fjdk sla;

;lkj fdsa ;lkj fdsa ;lkj fdsa ;lkj fdsa ;lkj fdsa ;lkj fdsa

asdf jkl; asdf jkl; asdf jkl; asdf jkl; asdf jkl; asdf jkl;

all; falls fad; dad; fall sad; fads dads ask; fad all; dad;

alas ask dads fads lass lad; sad; dad; fad; falls fall all;

a jaffa asks a lad; a lad asks; all lads ask; all dads ask;

alas a dad falls; all lads; ask dad; a jaffa fad; a sad lad

all dads ask alas; a jaffa fad; dad asks a lass; ask a lad;

all lads ask; a lass asks; a jaffa asks a lass; a jaffa fad

HOUR 2: e and i, g and h

e and i

Remember: Type the line, check, type again if you make a mistake. No delete key to be used.

♦ Use the d finger and take it up to the e
♦ Use the k finger and take it up to the i

ded; ede; ded; ede; ded; ede; ded; ede; ded; ede; ded; ede;

kik; iki; kik; iki; kik; iki; kik; iki; kik; iki; kik; iki;

feed seed deed lead deal seal leak seek feel keel leek less

kill fill dill sill jill kiss kill fill dill sill jill kiss

dad kisses jill; feed a lad; feed a lass; feed all; see all

a sad seal did fall; dad filled a field; a sill leaks alas;

a lad did lie; a lass is dead; feed a seal; feed a deaf lad;

feed a seal leeks; seek a lead; feed jill a leak; feel sad;

ask a deed; a sill leaks; jill falls ill; jaffa kisses jill

fill a seed field; ask less if jill is sad; all lasses fall

g and h

Remember: Type the line, check, type again if you make a mistake. No delete key to be used.

- Use the f finger and take it across to the g
- Use the j finger and take it across to the h

```
fgf; gfg; fgf; gfg; fgf; gfg; fgf; gfg; fgf; gfg; fgf; gfg;

jhj; hjh; jhj; hjh; jhj; hjh; jhj; hjh; jhj; hjh; jhj; hjh;

gas; has; gale hale gash hash gill hill gall hall geld held

high sigh hike like jig; dig; fig; gig; half heel lash dash

he liked a jig; she liked a jig; all liked a jig; see a jig

a lass sighed; see a high hill; has he held a seal; i asked

he held a jaffa as he fell; add a high gas; dig a fig field

i like a fig; half a heel has held; jill has a gash; i hike

jill digs a field; jill likes a hike; a gas leak kills all;

i sigh like jill; jed has a high hall; see jaffa as he jigs
```

Consolidation

Remember: Type the line, check, type again if you make a mistake. No delete key to be used.

fill a seed field; ask less if jill is sad; all lasses fall

ask a deed; a sill leaks; jill falls ill; jaffa kisses jill

feed a seal leeks; seek a lead; feed jill a leek; feel sad;

a lad did lie; a lass is dead; feed a seal; feed a deaf lad

a sad seal did fall; dad filled a field; a sill leaks alas;

dad kisses jill; feed a lad; feed a lass; feed all; see all

i sigh like jill; jed has a high hall; see jaffa as he jigs

jill digs a field; jill likes a hike; a gas leak kills all;

i like a fig; half a heel has held; jill has a gash; i hike

he held a jaffa as he fell; add a high gas; dig a fig field

a lass sighed; see a high hill; has he held a seal; i asked

he liked a jig; she liked a jig; all liked a jig; see a jig

HOUR 3: o and n, shift keys and t

o and n

Remember: Type the line, check, type again if you make a mistake. No delete key to be used.

◆ Use the l finger and take it up to the o
◆ Use the j finger and take it down to the n

lol; olo; lol; olo; lol; olo; lol; olo; lol; olo; lol; olo;

jnj; njn; jnj; njn; jnj; njn; jnj; njn; jnj; njn; jnj; njn;

dog; hog; fog; log; nog; jog; goon soon loon noon lose hose

nose dose none gone lone line fine dine sign nine lane sane

a lad had a fine dog; he held his lead; he jogged in a lane

fog had soon hidden all signs of a field; he fell on a log;

she had a fine salad and half of a fish; she soon had none;

he had a fine nose; she had gone insane; she had a fine fig

sad lad and his dog had gone jogging in a field and he fell

jed dosed on a log; he soon had no dog; he had gone inside;

Shift keys and t

Remember: Type the line, check, type again if you make a mistake. No delete key to be used.

- Use the little fingers for the shift keys. The shift keys are used for single capital letters. If you need to type lots of capitals, as in a heading, the caps lock key is better.
- Use the left little finger if typing a capital letter on the right side of the keyboard and the right little finger if typing a capital letter on the left side of the keyboard.
- Use the f finger and take it up to the t

Ask; See; Don; Fog; Gas; Had; Jag; Keg; Leg; Nag; All; Sag;

tag; tog; tin; ton; tan; ten; tea; tie; toll tall till tell

That Kill Fill Sell Till Hill Gill Doll Noel Tent Hide Tide

Lilt Hilt Silt Tilt Kilt Gilt Talk Gate Hate Fate Late Date

I said I hated the doll and that I felt it had a tin leg;

She talked of Noel and said she asked if he hated jogging

Ask to see Don and see if he sells gates; tents and dolls

I said I felt fine and that I jogged in a field at night;

He let his dog loose in the field and he fished in a lake

The fog had filled the field and I fell on a sagging log;

Consolidation

Remember: Type the line, check, type again if you make a mistake. No delete key to be used.

jed dosed on a log; he soon had no dog; he had gone inside;

the lad and his dog had gone jogging in a field and he fell

he had a fine nose; she had gone insane; she had a fine fig

she had a fine salad and half of a fish; she soon had none;

fog had soon hidden all signs of a field; he fell on a log;

a lad had a fine dog; he held his lead; he jogged in a lane

The fog had filled the field and I fell on a sagging log;

He let his dog loose in the field and he fished in a lake

I said I felt fine and that I jogged in a field at night;

Ask to see Don and see if he sells gates; tents and dolls

She talked of Noel and said she asked if he hated jogging

I said I hated the doll and that I felt it had a tin leg;

HOUR 4: extra practice . and y

Extra practice

Remember: Type the line, check, type again if you make a mistake. No delete key to be used.

A sad lad asks a lass; all dads fall alas; a jaffa falls

Dad asks a lad; alas a lass falls; Dad falls sad; a lass

Jill filled a field; Jill feeds a lass; Jill kisses Dad;

A lad killed a lass; a seal leaked alas; feed Dad seeds;

He likes a dig; she likes a dig; all liked a dig; a lass

Dad gashed his leg; a lad held a fig; see a jaffa field;

Half of a fish had hidden in the sea; she held his head;

She had no sign of the noon fog; The land had soon gone;

He talked of the fate of those dolls; I said I felt fine

She felt the fog lift late as she jogged into the field;

. and y

Remember: Type the line, check, type again if you make a mistake. No delete key to be used.

- ◆ Use the l finger and take it down to the .
- ◆ Use the j finger and take it up to the y.

```
hyn; yhn; nhy; hyn; yhn; nhy; hyn; yhn; nhy; hyn; yhn; nhy;
lo. ol. .lo lo. ol. .lo lo. ol. .lo lo. ol. .lo lo. ol. .lo
Yet. Yes. Yen. Nay. Hay. Gay. Say. Lay. Kay. Joy. Toy. Eye.
yell they flay slay yank yoke yolk toys eyes says nays lays
They all liked seeing the toys shining gaily on a shelf.
The lads yelled as they yanked the leg of a little lass.
I said that they yelled in joy at the toys on the shelf.
His eyes said it all. He talked of this feeling of hate.
The yolks of the little eggs lay shining in the toy tin.
Slay the nasty hog. Lay it on the shelf in the tool shed
```

Consolidation

Remember: Type the line, check, type again if you make a mistake. No delete key to be used.

She felt the fog lift late as she jogged into the field;

He talked of the fate of those dolls; I said I felt fine

She had no sign of the noon fog; The lane had soon gone;

Half of a fish had hidden in the sea; she held his head;

Dad gashed his leg; a lad held a fig; see a jaffa field;

He likes a dig; she likes a dig; all liked a dig; a lass

Slay the nasty hog. Lay it on the shelf in the tool shed

The yolks of the little eggs lay shining in the toy tin.

His eyes said it all. He talked of this feeling of hate.

I said that they yelled in joy at the toys on the shelf.

The lads yelled as they yanked the leg of a little lass.

They all liked seeing the toys shining gaily on a shelf.

**HOUR 5: , and w
r and b**

, and w

Remember: Type the line, check, type again if you make a mistake. No delete key to be used.

◆ Use the k finger and take it down to the ,
◆ Use the s finger and take it up to the w

ik, ,ki ki, ik, ,ki ki, ik, ,ki ki, ik, ,ki ki, ik, ,ki ki,

wsw sws wsw sws wsw sws wsw sws wsw sws wsw sws wsw sws wsw

way, was, wag, wan, wad, wet, wed, won, wok, wow, win, wig,

wall well will west wash wish wind wand when wean week weak

Ask the lady who was at the Dog Show to talk to the lad.

We talked, we walked, we went in to tea, then we waited.

We will wait while the lady talks to the tall, weak lad.

What was the lad doing, whistling at those wagging dogs.

We won the shiny toy, yet we did not win the tin shield.

Wash the wig, so that she will want to look at it again.

r and b

Remember: Type the line, check, type again if you make a mistake. No delete key to be used.

◆ Use the f finger and take it up to the r
◆ Use the f finger and take it down to the b

frf rfr frf rfr frf rfr frf rfr frf rfr frf rfr frf rfr frf

bgb gbg bgb gbg bgb gbg bgb gbg bgb gbg bgb gbg bgb gbg bgb

beat bear bead beak bean been beef bell bill bass bees boil

reel reef read reek roll rash rest root roof ride raid reed

There were lots of boys in the band and they enjoyed it.

The bread and rolls in the store had been there all day.

The bread baked in the kiln tasted better than the rest.

We had been riding the bikes all week and we were tired.

The bear reeked of beef stew so we beat a hasty retreat.

Billy had been rolling on the floor; he was boiling hot.

Consolidation

Remember: Type the line, check, type again if you make a mistake. No delete key to be used.

Wash the wig, so that she will want to look at it again.

We won the shiny toy, yet we did not win the tin shield.

What was the lad doing, whistling at those wagging dogs.

We will wait while the lady talks to the tall, weak lad.

We talked, we walked, we went in to tea, then we waited.

Ask the lady who was at the Dog Show to talk to the lad.

Billy had been rolling on the floor; he was boiling hot.

The bear reeked of beef stew so we beat a hasty retreat.

We had been riding the bikes all week and we were tired.

The bread baked in the kiln tasted better than the rest.

The bread and rolls in the store had been there all day.

There were lots of boys in the band and they enjoyed it.

HOUR 6: m and u
p and c

m and u

Remember: Type the line, check, type again if you make a mistake. No delete key to be used.

- Use the j finger and take it down to the m
- Use the j finger and take it up to the u

jmj mjm jmj mjm jmj mjm jmj mjm jmj mjm jmj mjm jmj mjm jmj

juj uju juj uju juj uju juj uju juj uju juj uju juj uju juj

mast mash mars mats mail meal mile mole moon mend mind mint

burn turn lure fuss dust rust must gust lust gush lush mush

My older brother kindly mended my new motor bike for me.

I must shut the toilet door and remember to use the key.

We must make our dinner more interesting and nourishing.

The wind gusted, and the mast blew around the main roof.

My mum mended the sagging hems. It was most kind of her.

The main meal of the day was roast beef and baked beans.

p and c

Remember: Type the line, check, type again if you make a mistake. No delete key to be used.

- ◆ Use the ; finger and take it up to the p
- ◆ Use the d finger and take it down to the c

;p; p;p ;p; p;p ;p; p;p ;p; p;p ;p; p;p ;p; p;p ;p; p;p ;p;

edc cdc edc cdc edc cdc edc cdc edc cdc edc cdc edc cdc edc

pool push pump purl pram prim pram palm peel pure paid pile

cart curt corn core cure care coal cash cell call clot clad

The policeman pushed his cycle by the tall church clock.

Appropriate care must be taken when photocopying papers.

The prim and proper nanny pushed the pram down the path.

Take care of the cash. Call David and pay him a portion.

Pull the pump up carefully and the water will spurt out.

The cart crashed past as it caught the edge of the path.

Consolidation

Remember: Type the line, check, type again if you make a mistake. No delete key to be used.

The main meal of the day was boiled beef and mushy peas.

My mum mended the sagging hems. It was most kind of her.

The wind gusted, and the mast blew around the main roof.

We must make our dinner more interesting and nourishing.

I must shut the toilet door and remember to use the key.

My older brother kindly mended my new motor bike for me.

The cart crashed past as it caught the edge of the path.

Pull the pump up carefully and the water will spurt out.

Take care of the cash. Call David and pay him a portion.

The prim and proper nanny pushed the pram down the path.

Appropriate care must be taken when photocopying papers.

The policeman pushed his cycle by the tall church clock.

HOUR 7: v and x
q and z

v and x

Remember: Type the line, check, type again if you make a mistake. No delete key to be used.

- ◆ Use the f finger and take it down to the v
- ◆ Use the s finger and take it down to the x

rfv vfv rfv vfv rfv vfv rfv vfv rfv vfv rfv vfv rfv vfv rfv

wsx xsw wsx xsw wsx xsw wsx xsw wsx xsw wsx xsw wsx xsw wsx

vent vein vane vine view vole vale veil vile vice vest vamp

oxen exit axis hoax taxi coax box, fox, cox, pox, fax, tax,

A vexed taxi man viewed the jam with extreme impatience.

The extra climb gave a better view over the next valley.

The exit was hidden from the view of the old van driver.

The fox jumped over the exit box and captured the voles.

It was a police hoax and the vice teams were very vexed.

Victoria views paying road taxes with very vivid hatred.

q and z

Remember: Type the line, check, type again if you make a mistake. No delete key to be used.

- Use the a finger and take it up to the q
- Use the a finger and take it down to the z

qaz aqa qaz aqa qaz aqa qaz aqa qaz aqa qaz aqa qaz aqa qaz

zaq aza zaq aza zaq aza zaq aza zaq aza zaq aza zaq aza zaq

aqua quit quay quid quod quiz quip quaint quota equal quell

zoom zeal zest haze maze gaze laze fuzz buzz zulu lazy hazy

Jo at the zoo asked quite odd questions about the zebra.

The lady gazed at the buzzing bee down by the boat quay.

He quit the jobs because he was a lazy and quiet worker.

In order to coax Xavier to eat he devised a quaint plan.

In the lazy, hazy days of summer it is quite often warm.

The buzzy bee zoomed around the lazy queen as she cried.

Consolidation

Remember: Type the line, check, type again if you make a mistake. No delete key to be used.

Victoria views paying road taxes with very vivid hatred.

It was a police hoax and the vice teams were very vexed.

The fox jumped over the exit box and captured the voles.

The exit was hidden from the view of the old van driver.

The extra climb gave a better view over the next valley.

A vexed taxi man viewed the jam with extreme impatience.

The buzzy bee zoomed around the lazy queen as she cried.

In the lazy, hazy days of summer it is quite often warm.

In order to coax Xavier to eat he devised a quaint plan.

He quit the jobs because he was a lazy and quiet worker.

The lady gazed at the buzzing bee down by the boat quay.

Jo at the zoo asked quite odd questions about the zebra.

HOUR 8: sentence drills

Sentence drills

Remember: Type the line, check, type again if you make a mistake. No delete key to be used.

A An old man had a fall and banged his head hard.

B Buy a ball for Beth and bring it back in a bag.

C Call the computer company to cancel collection.

D Did I decorate the dining room during December.

E Every evening after tea he went to see Georgie.

F Fill a fat frog with food from the first floor.

G Get a good grip on the gate, and drag it along.

H Have a happy holiday at Hastings Hall in March.

I I will fill it with a lining first to insulate.

J Just ask Jane to judge the jitterbug and tango.

K The kind king gave back a kettle to the tinker.

L Linda lost her silver locket at Looe last year.

M   Some men made a magnificent machine from metal.

N   No new newspapers need to be sent to Ned today.

O   Clive opted to organise the food on the outing.

P   Please pack the pots into paper packs promptly.

Q   Queenie requested varied questions in the quiz.

R   Ronald ran a race to raise revenue for charity.

S   Show us some sea shells and shiny silver stars.

T   The toy teddy was fixed to the top of the tree.

U   The undergraduate undertook to shut up the box.

V   Very enviable views were seen from the village.

W   We got wet when we went walking near the woods.

X   The extra anxious taxi man was extremely vexed.

Y   They say they should pay for the toy by cheque.

Z   A bee buzzed lazily as it zoomed round the zoo.

HOUR 9: figures

Figures

Remember: Type the line, check, type again if you make a mistake. No delete key to be used.

de3ed de3d d3d de3ed de3d d3d de3ed de3d d3d de3ed de3d

ju7uj ju7j j7j ju7uj ju7j j7j ju7uj ju7j j7j ju7uj ju7j

fr4rf fr4f f4f fr4rf fr4f f4f fr4rf fr4f f4f fr4rf fr4f

ki8ik ki8k k8k ki8ik ki8k k8k ki8ik ki8k k8k ki8ik ki8k

aq1qa aq1a a1a aq1qa aq1a a1a aq1qa aq1a a1a aq1qa aq1a

sw2ws sw2s s2s sw2ws sw2s s2s sw2ws sw2s s2s sw2ws sw2s

jy6yj jy6j j6j jy6yj jy6j j6j jy6yj jy6j j6j jy6yj jy6j

fr5rf fr5f f5f fr5rf fr5f f5f fr5rf fr5f f5f fr5rf fr5f

lo9ol lo9l l9l lo9ol lo9l l9l lo9ol lo9l l9l lo9ol lo9l

;p0p; ;p0; ;0; ;p0p; ;p0; ;0; ;p0p; ;p0; ;0; ;p0p; ;p0;

1qaz 2wsx 3edc 4rfv 5tgb 6yhn 7ujm 8ik, 9ol. 0p;/ 1qaz.

zaq1 xsw2 cde3 vfr4 bgt5 nhy6 mju7 ,ki8 .lo9 /;p0 zaq1.

3 duds 33 dots 3 dons 33 dogs 3 duds 33 dots 3 dons 33 dogs

7 jugs 77 jars 7 jams 77 jigs 7 jugs 77 jars 7 jams 77 jigs

4 figs 44 feet 4 fees 44 fans 4 figs 44 feet 4 fees 44 fans

8 kits 88 keys 8 kids 88 kegs 8 kits 88 keys 8 kids 88 kegs

This job lot was: 11 woollen suits, 1 blouse and 11 collars

2 saws 22 sons 2 suns 22 sets 2 saws 22 sons 2 suns 22 sets

6 jays 66 jobs 6 jets 66 jabs 6 jays 66 jobs 6 jets 66 jabs

5 fins 55 fibs 5 fags 55 firs 5 fins 55 fibs 5 fags 55 firs

9 logs 99 lads 9 lots 99 laws 9 logs 99 lads 9 lots 99 laws

20 pages; 30 pills; 40 papers 20 pages; 30 pills; 40 papers

The man caught 26 pike, 15 roach, 36 tiddlers and 2 plaice.

Jane got 16 marks in geography and just 14 marks in French.

Consolidation

Remember: Type the line, check, type again if you make a mistake. No delete key to be used.

There were 3 dogs, 33 cats, and 330 hamsters at the park.

I saw 7 people on Monday, 77 on Tuesday, and 7 yesterday.

Weigh out 4 oz of flour, 4 oz of sugar, and add the eggs.

At 8 o'clock I went out to see the 88 horses at the show.

I had 1 suit, 1 pair of trousers, 1 skirt and 11 jumpers.

The 2 of us saw 2 plays at the theatre on the 22nd August.

If you add 6 and 6 and 6 you will find the right answers.

I think 5 is a nice round figure; 5 people and 5 animals.

On the 9th September we went out at 9 pm in 9 cranky cars.

The value is 0, but we really need a value of 100 or 200.

Jane had 239 bars of chocolate, 56 lollies and 76 sweets.

Add 569 to the totals of 890 and then you will have 1459.

HOUR 10: alphabetical paragraphs

Alphabetical paragraphs

Remember: Type the paragraph, check, type again if you make a mistake. No delete key to be used.

The amazing monkey scampered quickly over the floor of the cage. He was very excited as his keeper was just about to feed him.

The extra homework given to the children did not keep them quiet and they jumped about the desks with ferocious zeal.

Jenny Pope was a fun loving, likeable girl. She amazed everyone with her quiet, but extremely considerate nature.

The excellent marks achieved by the student justly proved he was not lazy and that he was, in fact, really quite knowledgeable.

Send a telex to the Manager of the Zoo quoting the prices given in July for the supply of animal feed. The Zoo Keeper is urgently waiting for the information to be sent to him.

The girl quivered with fear as she watched the blaze. A bomb had exploded just outside the store where she had been shopping only a few moments earlier. She wondered if anyone had been killed.

Up until extra time had been played, the footballer performed in quite a remarkable way. He zoomed in on every shot and almost scored a goal. He justly deserved the praise given to him.

PART 2
ADDITIONAL TOUCH TYPING
PRACTICE MATERIAL

Sentence Practice

Sentence practice

Remember: Type the line, check, type again if you make a mistake. No delete key to be used.

A Agatha Attwall added an attraction to the acrobatic act.

   Alan saw an animal across the Avenue. It was a big cat.

B Bundle up the boxes by the bin and Billie will buy them.

   Barbara bounced the bats and balls across the boulevard.

C Catch the crafty cat as he creeps across the curtaining.

   Cook the crumbly cod bake in the Cannone cooker quickly.

D Dad did his usual good deed dividing the cod decisively.

   Did Danny deliver the dodgy DVD players to Darren today.

E Every television programme entertains us to some extent.

   Erica Enever lives in the village close to The Elephant.

Sentence practice

Remember: Type the line, check, type again if you make a mistake. No delete key to be used.

F   Find a fat frog and float it in the fast flowing stream.

    Frank felt that he fought a fierce battle with Felicity.

G   George got gold in the Olympics and a gilt gong in Peru.

    Give the gift to Geraldine. She is a gifted, good girl.

H   Harry has his hammer and his hacksaw handy at all times.

    He hesitated and held a hand up to halt the hitchhikers.

I   In his haste he instigated the idea irrespective of her.

    I invited Ivy to join me in Iceland to visit my parents.

J   John and Jan judged the juggling competition in January.

    Just join in and enjoy the javelin throwing at St Johns.

Sentence practice

Remember: Type the line, check, type again if you make a mistake. No delete key to be used.

K   Kathy and Kirsty kept kicking each other as they walked.

    Keep a close eye on Kitty. Make sure she keeps her key.

L   Let Lucy live in that lucky little house by the library.

    Let me type you a letter listing all the past loopholes.

M   My mother made me mend my musical mat and then make tea.

    Milly Mollie Mandy made many new friends at the mansion.

N   Ned and Nancy knew they needed to be together all night.

    Knit a nice sweater for Nancy to wear at the Barn Dance.

O   Olive often opted for an old book rather than a new one.

    Go down to the office and look for the file I have lost.

Sentence practice

Remember: Type the line, check, type again if you make a mistake. No delete key to be used.

P   Peter Piper picked a peppercorn and put it on his plate.

    Pack the pies into a paper packet and post them to Paul.

Q   Queenie quoted the quiet kind gentleman from Queensland.

    The quiz show was quite busy and received many requests.

R   Ring Rose to remind her of the Rolls Royce car on offer.

    Robert rolled down the road regretting his recklessness.

S   See Simon and ask if he is singing in Selby on Saturday.

    Sarah stayed outside as her sister sat inside on a seat.

T   Take the train to Taunton to paint the tantalising view.

    Trusty Tim told Tina that he caught the terrible tinker.

Sentence practice

Remember: Type the line, check, type again if you make a mistake. No delete key to be used.

U Turn up at four today and you will not need to rush out.

Up until then Ursula had been unaware of the shy butler.

V Victor Vasey lived up to his nickname of Viking Viceroy.

Victoria lived in Liverpool with a view over the Mersey.

W Willy Wonka was a wonderful character who was in a book.

We wondered where William was. He wandered up the road.

X Extreme exercise can cause much exertion and exhaustion.

Extra examinations can help Mary to exceed expectations.

Y If you yearn to play the oboe you have to try very hard.

Yelling at the young child did not please Mandy Claydon.

Sentence practice

Remember: Type the line, check, type again if you make a mistake. No delete key to be used.

Z   In the lazy hazy days of summer, Suzannah zoomed around.

   Zak and Zoe visited the zoo and liked seeing the zebras.

1-5 Please ask for 1 tie, 2 shirts, 3 jackets and 4 jumpers.

   He had to put 55 pies in with the 3 pasties and 2 flans.

1-5 Adam scored 4 goals, had 23 near misses and 2 penalties.

   The recipe asked for 14 oz sugar, 5 oz flour, 3 oz marg.

6-10 We needed 6 cars, 8 motor bikes and 10 scooters to race.

   George scored 689, Alan scored 786 and Peter scored 876.

6-10 Amy bought 16 lollies, 18 sherbets and 9 chocolate bars.

   The A868 road to Hull passes close to the A968 and A789.

Paragraph Practice

Paragraph practice

Remember: Type the paragraph, check, type again if you make a mistake. No delete key to be used.

Christopher Jones handled the motor car extremely well. He was a quick driver and he went from zero to sixty in no time at all, but he did seem to know what he was doing and I always felt safe at his side.

The bee buzzed around the violet flowers. It was quite brightly coloured and it made a lot of noise. I had just started using my rake nearby, but as I am afraid of bees I had to stop until it buzzed away.

Jacqueline had been entered for the relay race. She was a pretty, zealous young thing, but her running was extremely slow and the other members of the team were not very pleased with her efforts to bring them luck.

Paragraph practice

Remember: Type the paragraph, check, type again if you make a mistake. No delete key to be used.

It was just an amazing and appalling day.   It had started quietly enough, but then all hell broke loose.   Things were not back to normal until the evening.   By then we had experienced quite enough excitement for one day.

When all is said and done, Zoe could not have behaved any better.   She knew when to extract the information from him, but just as she was about to do so, he collapsed on the floor.   She quickly got to him but it was too late.

All around the park people were enjoying themselves.   It was a lazy sort of day, quite warm and pleasant.   Children played excitedly on the swings, climbing frame and slides. Everyone seemed to be happy and content.

Paragraph practice

Remember: Type the paragraph, check, type again if you make a mistake. No delete key to be used.

At the Annual General Meeting the Chairman stated that the full quota of money had been used and that an exceptionally small amount was still available in reserve stock. He said there was no place for laziness if the company was to survive.

We all went out to play with our kites. It was a lovely day. All was quiet and calm until we started zooming around at great speed. We did enjoy ourselves. After the exercise we felt we needed a bath.

Sally was taken to Quaser for her fifteenth birthday treat. It was a cold day in the middle of January and everyone was extremely glad to get inside in the warm. They played three games and then went next door to have tea.

Paragraph practice

Remember: Type the paragraph, check, type again if you make a mistake. No delete key to be used.

Zak was a very good boy. He looked quite small and frail, but he made up for it with his strength of character. I enjoyed his excellent company a lot. He was good fun and very polite.

Jane felt very lazy that day. She had seen a wonderful but scary film the night before and it had quite exhausted her. Her back ached and she had a painful headache. She decided to take things easy.

Jim's memory of the event was very hazy. He had received quite a crack on the head and for a while he had been unconscious. It took him a good few weeks to get over it and even then he often felt sick and suffered from headaches. He looked very waxy and pale.

Paragraph practice

Remember: Type the paragraph, check, type again if you make a mistake. No delete key to be used.

On Boxing Day last year we all went out to see the pantomime. It was very enjoyable, particularly the clowns who zoomed about the auditorium on their cycles. We were quite tired when we got home and spent a lazy evening in front of the black and white television.

Katy and Jacqueline caught the shoplifter just as he was about to leave the department store. They were very excited when they told me about it, and I felt quite dazed by their account of events.

I am going on holiday to France in August. I am already getting very excited about it and hope to spend a lazy two weeks touring around the quiet countryside of Provence and Jura. I hope the weather will be kind to me.

Paragraph practice

Remember: Type the paragraph, check, type again if you make a mistake. No delete key to be used.

When I make a fruit cake I use 8 oz of flour, 6 oz of margarine, 5 oz of sugar, 18 oz of mixed dried fruit, 2 tablespoons of marmalade, 2 oz of glace cherries, 4 eggs and 1 tablespoon of milk.

When we went to the zoo we saw 6 alligators, 25 monkeys, 18 kangaroos, 25 elephants and 64 lions. We were disappointed in the number of tigers as there were only 15 on display out of a possible 30.

Please ask Mickey to process my order. I would like 6 bags of sugar, 4 bags of self raising flour, 10 tins of baked beans, 4 tins of chicken soup and 15 tins of tuna. Could he please deliver it on 20 February 2007.

Longer Practice Pieces

The passages on the following pages are longer
and will take more concentration.

Type each piece, checking carefully at the end
and correcting where necessary.

Print out your work and keep a copy in a
file to show your progress.

Remember: use your hand chart if
necessary, but under no circumstances
should you look at the keys.

Task 1

There are many opportunities available for a good secretary. A company will be only too pleased to promote a secretary to personal assistant or even higher if she has proved to be capable of more responsibility. The appointment to a higher position may be subject to a reference from the person's present boss, who should make sure the necessary information is received prior to interview by whoever is concerned with interviewing for the promotion.

The more a company offers to its employees, the more it should expect to receive in return. I believe sufficient thought should be given to developing a structure of promotion which will apply to all.

Task 2

The hotel industry has suffered from the present recession just the same as everywhere else. Ordinary people no longer have as much money to spend and businesses are curtailing the activities of their reps and senior staff. Hotels have to try to compete with one another for their share of the market. It is said, however, that next year should see an upturn in the economy.

Task 3

The Fortune Hotel is one of a group of hotels owned by the Broker Group. It is set in the midst of East Anglia, near to the coast and the Norfolk Broads. The surrounding countryside shows rural England in the very best light. The town of Holt has a character all of its own. Many individual specialist shops sell a wide variety of goods and the Georgian facade of the buildings is an extra attraction. Every shopping need is catered for here, and back at The Fortune, every comfort is provided for your East Anglian holiday or business visit. We are sure that when you leave you will take home many pleasant memories.

Task 3 continued

THE COUNTRY BAR

The Country Bar at The Fortune Hotel offers residents and non-residents an opportunity to relax in a restful, friendly atmosphere. The decor is designed to produce a feeling of well-being and tranquillity. No expense has been spared in supplying the lavish upholstery and curtains. All in all, the Country Bar is the place to be.

Task 4

STARTING A NEW JOB

Points to Remember

Arrive early and report to the person you have been asked to see.

Take a notebook and pencil with you and make notes on anything relevant you are told on that first day. Although you might think you will remember you probably will not.

Try to be friendly to everyone. Make a mental note of names as you are introduced to people.

Always ask if you are given something to do that you do not understand. A person who has performed a particular task for many years will not stop to think that you might find it hard to pick up at first.

Do not panic if everything goes wrong on your first day. Give it time and all will be well in the end.

Task 5

THE FORTUNE HOTEL, HOLT, NORFOLK

Set in beautiful East Anglian countryside, The Fortune offers the perfect combination of peace and quiet with excellent amenities.

ROSE BOWL RESTAURANT

Our Restaurant is well-known throughout the area for its fine cuisine and appealing décor. Meals are reasonably priced, and on a Saturday night dinner can be combined with dancing in the Pullman Suite afterwards.

PULLMAN SUITE

Apart from our regular dances, the Pullman Suite is available for private hire. It has its own bar and a superb dance floor. We can arrange a band or disco, or you can provide your own.

COUNTRY BAR

If you like a quiet drink in a restful atmosphere, or perhaps a light snack at lunchtime, then the Country Bar is the place to be.

Task 6

ANNUAL CHARITY FUN DAY

The Fortune Hotel is planning to hold its fourth Annual Charity Fun Day on 1 August 20—, commencing at 1100 hrs.

Admission is £2.00 for adults and £1.00 for children under 14.

This year all proceeds will go to Cancer Research. Even the professional acts are giving their services free of charge, so we hope to make as much as possible for this worthy cause.

There will be a variety of stalls. There will also be a bouncy castle, pony rides, full catering facilities and a car boot sale.

All the facilities of the hotel will be available to everyone for the day, including the swimming pool, although an extra charge will be made for this.

Tickets are available now, direct from the hotel. Admission will be by advance ticket only, so make sure of yours now as numbers are limited.

The Fortune Hotel's Charity Fun Day should prove to be the best local event of the year. See you there!

Task 7

CURRICULUM VITAE

Many job advertisements today ask for a Curriculum Vitae to be sent by way of application. A Curriculum Vitae actually means the course of your life. The term is frequently shortened to CV. Your CV should contain personal details such as date of birth, address, nationality, interests etc, as well as details of your education, examination results and any past job experience. If you have worked in the holidays mention this too. It should also contain the names and addresses of two referees, one of whom should be your present or past employer. If you have not been employed before, give the names of two people who have known you for a long time and can at least vouch for your character. Your Headteacher would be a good place to start. Whoever you give as referees, do remember to ask them first as this is common courtesy.

Write out your CV in rough first, amend where necessary, and then produce the final copy. It is worth taking the time and trouble to prepare a neat and accurate CV. It is the first point of contact with your prospective employer, and even if you are not experienced, a neat and tidy, well-presented CV will impress. Obviously, as you gain more qualifications or job experience you should amend your CV accordingly.

Accompanying your CV should be a brief covering letter explaining where you saw the advertisement and why you are interested in the vacancy.

Task 8

INTERVIEW TECHNIQUE

If your CV impresses your prospective employer, you will receive a letter or telephone call asking you to attend for interview. Assuming you accept this invitation, you can help yourself by doing a little research in advance. Find out what you can about the company in question, what they do, how many employees etc. Make sure you know where their offices are, and find out about transport times if you are not travelling by car. If necessary do a 'trial run' first to check how long the journey takes.

When you attend the interview you should arrive just two or three minutes early. Earlier than that and you will probably coincide with the applicant scheduled before you. <u>Never</u> arrive late. You will give a bad impression – the employer will assume you will always arrive late should you be employed by the company. Wear clothes that are smart and clean, but do not dress up to the extent that you feel uncomfortable. <u>Never</u> wear jeans.

First impressions count for a lot, so make them as good as you can. If you feel nervous, remember that the interviewer may feel nervous too, after all she or he is a human being just as you are. The important thing is not to let your nerves get the better of you. Try to keep calm and answer all questions put to you as well as you are able. Sound interested in what the interviewer is saying and try to contribute enough information for him or her to see that you would be suitable for the position on offer. When you are asked if you have any questions, make sure you can think of something to ask – it shows you have been listening.

When the interview is over, remember to thank the interviewer for his or her time.

Usually a successful applicant for a job is notified fairly quickly, either by letter or telephone; you could even be told straight away.

Good luck at interviews and in finding your dream job – or at least as near as you can get to it!

Task 9

SECURITY

<u>Visitors Book</u>

All guests <u>must</u> sign the Visitors Book on arrival, stating their name, address, and date and time of arrival. When checking out of the Hotel, the date and time of departure should be inserted.

<u>Valuables</u>

The Hotel accepts no responsibility for valuables left in rooms. A safe is available for guests' use and no charge is made for this service. Please ask at Reception for details.

<u>Theft</u>

In the unlikely event that a guest notices any item missing from his or her room, this should be reported immediately, either to Reception or to the Hotel Manager.

<u>Main Entrance Closure</u>

The Hotel's Main Entrance and Reception will be closed from midnight to 0700 hrs each night for reasons of security. Guests requiring access during these times should ring the bell at the Main Entrance and inform the Night Porter of their name and room number. As long as he is satisfied, access will be granted.

<u>General Awareness</u>

Guests should, at all times, look after their property and not leave bags and cases lying around in Reception or corridors. They should also immediately report any suspicious packages they see to Reception or a member of staff. Any person suspected of theft will be questioned by the Manager and, if necessary, referred to the Police.

Task 10

REPORT ON VISIT TO THE GEORGE HOTEL

I recently visited the George Hotel with the main aim of finding ways to improve our reception area. This was the first time I had been to the George since the opening of their new reception area in 2000.

My first impression was of a bright and welcoming entrance hall and reception desk, with elegant and comfortable furniture. The actual reception desk was much larger than ours, and housed many leaflets of local interest, as well as full information on all aspects of the hotel! There were two receptionists on duty and they both wore smart uniforms – much more up-to-date than our own.

Specific points of operation were as follows:

Guests are greeted at the door by a porter who introduces himself and then escorts them to the reception desk.

The receptionist books the guests in and gives them some verbal information on the facilities of the hotel. She then makes sure they have the opportunity to collect the relevant literature from the reception desk.

A porter escorts the guests to their room.

Arrangements for paper delivery, alarm calls etc, are made afterwards when either one of the porters or a receptionist visits the guests personally in their room approximately one hour after arrival and checks that everything is in order. At that time any special requests can be noted. Obviously, in addition, room service and telephone contact is available twenty-four hours a day.

A table has been prepared showing differences between our two hotels. I feel that certain of their policies should be implemented at The Fortune when we make our changes next year. Another visit nearer the time could decide specific ways to make improvements.

PART 3
MICROSOFT WORD THEORY

An Introduction to Word 2007

Microsoft Word is a software program that helps you produce professional looking documents with the minimum amount of time and trouble. The instructions in this book are based on **Word 2007**.

Before opening **Word** and working on it for the first time you will need to know how to use and control your mouse. Practise resting your hand on the mouse, and use your thumb and two right fingers to move the mouse on your desk. Use your remaining fingers to press the mouse buttons.

There are four main mouse actions:

1   Click by pressing and releasing the left mouse button. This is what you will use most.

2   Double click by quickly pressing and releasing the left mouse button twice.

3   Right click by pressing and releasing the right mouse button.

4   Drag by positioning the mouse pointer over an object on your screen and then pressing and holding down the left mouse button. Still holding down the button, move the mouse to where you want to place the object and then release the button.

Running Word

The operating system is called **Microsoft Windows** and the version used in this book is **Windows Vista**. In order to begin using **Word** you will need to move through this operating system by left clicking on the circular **Start** button at the bottom left of your opening screen. Push the mouse pointer up to **All Programs**, and then look for **Microsoft Office**. Move through the list of programs in **Office** and you will see **Microsoft Office Word 2007**. Left click and the **Word** opening screen will arrive.

Word offers five ways to view your document. Most of the time it is best to use **Print Layout View**, but to explain further:

Print Layout View – This is the view shown on the next page. This view displays your document as it will appear on a printed page. The Print Layout View displays margins, headers, footers and page numbers.

Full Screen Reading - This view is useful if you are opening a document primarily to read it as it optimizes the reading experience and the pages are designed to fit well on your screen.

Web Layout View – This view displays your document as it will appear on the Web. The Web Layout View is useful when you are using Word to create a Web page.

Outline View – This view helps you review and work with the structure of your document. The Outline View lets you collapse a document to see only the main headings, or expand a document to see all the main headings and text. This is useful when working with large documents.

Draft - This view simplifies your document so that you can quickly enter, edit and format text. The Draft View does not display margins, headers, footers or page numbers.

The **View** buttons are found at the bottom right hand of your screen. If you click on each one in turn you will see the difference between them. It is best if you have a document open before you do this, so that the changes are more apparent.

The Opening Screen

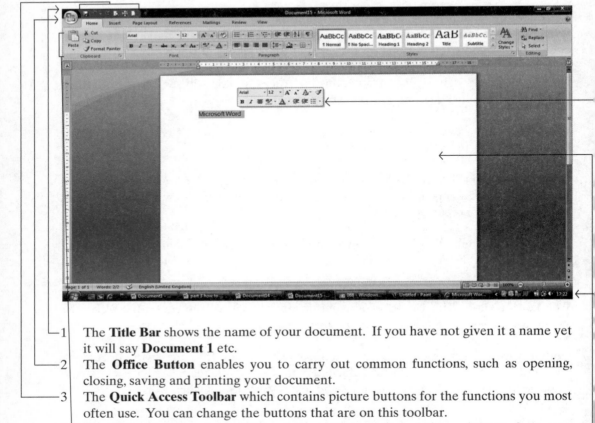

1   The **Title Bar** shows the name of your document. If you have not given it a name yet it will say **Document 1** etc.

2   The **Office Button** enables you to carry out common functions, such as opening, closing, saving and printing your document.

3   The **Quick Access Toolbar** which contains picture buttons for the functions you most often use. You can change the buttons that are on this toolbar.

4   The **Ribbon Bar** has seven different tabs with a number of picture buttons for you to click on.

5   The **Main Window** is the area of your screen in which you type.

6   The **Status Bar** shows what page you are on, how many pages there are in the document and how many words you have typed.

7   The **Mini Toolbar** appears when you highlight text and enables you to use common formatting features, such as adding bold or underlining.

Selecting Commands Using The Office Button
Click on the circular Office Button. Click on the command you require. Some commands have further options; these can be displayed by clicking on the ▶ button to the right of the command.

Selecting Commands Using the Quick Access Toolbar
Click on the button for the command you wish to use.

Selecting Commands Using The Ribbon Bar
The Ribbon Bar is comprised of seven tabs. To move to a different tab, click on the tab name.

Tab labels

Group labels — Click here to open the full menu for the group

Within each tab there are different groups – for example, the Home tab has Clipboard, Font, Paragraph, Styles and Editing groups. To use a command displayed in one of the groups on the tab, click on the button assigned to the command. To open up the full menu for each group, click on the box in the bottom right hand corner of that group.

Some of the command buttons are explained on these pages.

Office Button

NEW BLANK DOCUMENT. Gives you a new piece of paper.

OPEN. Shows the files and folders on the drive you are working in.

SAVE. Saves the active file with its current file name and location.

SAVE AS. Saves the active file with a different file name and/or location.

PRINT. Prints out your document.

PREPARE. Prepares the document for distribution.

E-MAIL. Can send the document as an e-mail message.

PUBLISH. Distributes the document to others.

CLOSE. Closes the active file.

Quick Access Toolbar

UNDO. Reverses your last action or actions.

REDO. Reverses your undo action.

The Home Tab on the Ribbon Bar

CUT. Removes selected text from a document and puts it in the clipboard.

COPY. Copies selected text to the clipboard.

PASTE. Inserts cut or copied piece of text into your document.

FORMAT PAINTER. Copies format of a selected piece of text and applies it to the text or object you click on.

FONT. Changes the font of the selected text.

FONT SIZE. Changes the size of the selected text.

GROW FONT. Increases the size of the text.

SHRINK FONT. Decreases the size of the text.

CLEAR FORMATTING. Removes all formatting from selected text, leaving plain, black text.

BOLD. Adds or removes bold type to selected text.

ITALIC. Adds or removes italic type to selected text.

UNDERLINE. Adds or removes underline to selected text. Clicking on the ▼ arrow will allow you to choose different underline styles.

STRIKETHROUGH. Adds a line through the middle of selected text.

SUBSCRIPT. Adds small letters or numbers below the text.

SUPERSCRIPT. Adds small letters or numbers above the text.

CHANGE CASE. Changes the case of the text to or from capitals. Clicking on the ▼ arrow will display further options.

HIGHLIGHT. Marks text so it is highlighted and stands out. Clicking on the ▼ arrow will allow you to choose the colour for the highlight.

FONT COLOUR. Formats the selected text with a different colour. The colour can be chosen by clicking on the ▼ arrow.

BULLETS. Adds bullets to/removes bullets from selected text.

NUMBERING. Adds numbers to/removes numbers from selected text.

MULTILEVEL LIST. Adds a multileveled list of bullets/numbers to text.

DECREASE INDENT. Indents selected text to previous tab stop.

INCREASE INDENT. Indents selected text to next tab stop.

SORT. Sorts text by letter of the alphabet or number.

SHOW/HIDE. Displays formatting marks such as tab characters, paragraph marks and hidden text.

ALIGN LEFT. Aligns text to the left with a ragged right edge.

CENTRE. Centres the text.

ALIGN RIGHT. Aligns text to the right with a ragged left edge.

JUSTIFY. Aligns selected text to both left and right margins.

LINE SPACING. Allows you to select the line spacing for your document.

SHADING. Applies a background colour behind the text or in a table.

BORDERS. Applies a line or full border to text or in a table.

Allows you to pick a style for the text you are typing.

CHANGE STYLES. Allows you to change the set of styles used in the document.

FIND. Finds a particular word or set of words in the document.

REPLACE. Finds a particular word or set of words in the document and replaces them with another word or set of words.

SELECT. Selects particular text or objects in the document.

The Basics of Using Microsoft Word

Preparing, Saving and Printing a Document.

To begin typing, if you do not have a white screen showing, click on the **New** button in the **Office Button** menu and **Create** to start a blank document. You will see an insertion point on your screen. The text that you type will appear where the insertion point flashes. Type the text for your document. As your text reaches the end of each line it will automatically 'wrap round' to the next line. You need only to press the **Enter** key when you want to start a new paragraph, and to leave a gap between paragraphs.

If you make a mistake as you type you can correct this in one of two ways: the backspace delete key (on the figure row, a large key with an arrow on it) will delete text to the left of the insertion point. The **Delete** key will delete text to the right of the insertion point.

Word automatically underlines spelling errors in red, grammar errors in green and 'inconsistent formatting' in blue. Common spelling/typing errors are corrected automatically as you type, but if a red, green or blue line appears, right click on the word or phrase and a suggested solution should be forthcoming. Unfortunately, Word will underline any word that it does not recognise, so don't assume that every word underlined in red will be an error. Alternatively you can leave your spell checking until the end of your document and then click on the **Spelling and Grammar** button in the **Review** tab. You can select or ignore the suggestions as required.

Once you have finished your document you should save it. Click on the **Save** button in the **Quick Access Toolbar** or use the **Save** command in the **Office Button** menu. Make sure you are saving in the right place eg, **Documents** and where it says **File name** give your document a name. If your document is likely to be read on another computer and you do not know if the computer has Word 2007 on it then in **Save as type** you can choose **Word 97-2003 Document.** This is necessary because Word 2007 documents cannot be opened on earlier versions of Word. Click on **Save** in the bottom right hand corner.

Finally you can print out your document. There are two ways of doing this. The easy way is to click on the picture of the printer on the **Quick Access Toolbar.** Alternatively click on **Print** in the **Office Button** menu and bring up the print menu. This gives you more options such as multiple copies, selected pages only etc. Make your choice and click **OK.**

When your document has been saved and printed you can click on **Close** in the **Office Button** menu to file it away. If you want to find it again, click on **Open** in the **Office Button** menu and your file should be listed.

FILES AND FOLDERS

All the documents you save on your computer are referred to as **files**. As you use your computer more and more, you will need to keep your work organised so that you can go to it quickly. **Files** are organised by saving them into **folders**. One very important **Folder** that is set up automatically for you is **Documents**. This is where Windows expects you to create your own subfolders to store your work. With Word, **Files** are shown as small blue squares with a 'W' inside and **Folders** are shown as oblong yellow shapes.

Getting Help

If you want some help with carrying out a task, you can use **Microsoft Office Word Help**. This can be accessed by pressing F1 on your keyboard, or by clicking on the question mark in the top right hand corner of the screen.

Selecting Text

Position the mouse over the first word you want to select. Click and drag the mouse over the text.

Using Bold, Italic and Underline

There are two ways of doing this. Either:
Click on the appropriate button on the **Home** tab of the **Ribbon Bar** before typing the text, and then click again to deselect when you have finished.
Or
Type the text first. Then select the appropriate word or words and click on the appropriate button on the **Ribbon Bar** or **Mini Toolbar**.

Changing the Case of Text

You can change the case of text in your document without the need to retype. To do this:
Select the text you want to change.
Click on the **Change Case** button **Aa▾** on the **Home** tab of the **Ribbon Bar** and select the case you require.

Centreing Text

Either: click on the **Centre** button on the **Home** tab of the **Ribbon Bar**, and then click on the **Align Left** button when you have finished.
Or: type the text first, select it and click on the **Centre** button on either the **Ribbon Bar** or **Mini Toolbar.**

Moving or Copying Text

You can move or copy text to a new location in your document by using the buttons on the **Home** tab of the **Ribbon Bar**. You can copy many items into the **Clipboard**, enabling you to hold information and enter it into various documents as and when you are ready to do so.

Moving Text
Moving text means to physically move a block of text from one place to another. The text disappears from its original place in your document.

Copying Text
Copying text means to leave the text where it is and put it somewhere else as well, so it appears in two places.

To do either of these:
Select the text you want to move or copy.

Click on one of the following buttons: ✂ Cut 📋 Copy

Click the location where you want to place the text.

Click on **Paste** to place the text in the new location.

Indenting Paragraphs

Three indents sit at the left of the ruler line and one sits at the right. They are shown as two triangles and a rectangle on the left and a triangle on the right. You can use the indents to make paragraphs in your documents stand out. The options you have are as follows:

▽ The top triangle is the 'first line indent'. Left click with the mouse and drag the indent to where you want it to be. Press the tab key to move across to it.

△ The bottom triangle is the 'hanging indent'. This indents all but the first line of the paragraph to the right. It is very useful for numbered paragraphs. To use the 'hanging indent' for numbered paragraphs:

- ◆ Type the number at the margin.
- ◆ Left click with the mouse and drag the indent to where you want it to be.
- ◆ Press the tab key to move across to it.
- ◆ This will indent the second and subsequent lines under the first, but you can still go

back to the margin for number 2, 3, etc.

Look at the following example using a 'hanging indent'.

1   What is the Internet and what does it have to offer? We start at the beginning and show you how easy it is to get connected.

☐   The rectangle is the 'left indent'. This will indent all the text from the left margin, as in this example here. We can use the 'left indent' with the corresponding 'right indent' which is at the right-hand side of the ruler line. For both, you left click and drag as before.

This text has been indented using the left and right indent.

Inserting Symbols

It is very possible that you will want to insert a symbol in your documents from time to time. Examples are:

To insert a symbol:

◆   Click on where you want the symbol to appear in your document.
◆   Click on the **Insert** tab on the **Ribbon Bar**. Click on **Symbol**. The symbol dialogue box appears displaying the symbols for the current font. Click on the down arrow by **Font** to display additional symbols. Click on the font you want to display.
◆   Click on the symbol you want to place in your document. Click on **Insert** and then **Close** to return to your document.
◆   If your symbol does not look big enough, highlight it and change the font size.

Note: In the examples above, the symbols on the first line were found in **Normal Text**. The symbols in the second line were found in **Wingdings** and the symbols in the third line were found in **Wingdings 2.**

Line Spacing

On Word 2007 there is a button on the **Home** tab of the **Ribbon Bar**, next to the alignment buttons. It has a double headed arrow on it and if you click on the down arrow you can choose your line spacing from the available options.

Changing the Alignment of Text

You can enhance the appearance of your document by aligning the text in different ways.

You can right align text like this:

Waveney Secretarial School
Dorlen House

You can centre text like this:

Waveney Secretarial School
Dorlen House

You can left align text like this:
Waveney Secretarial School
Dorlen House

Or you can fully justify text like this:

We are a small, independently run School, offering day and evening classes in computer skills. Our successful teaching policy is based on individual tuition in a friendly atmosphere. We are a City and Guilds examination centre which means you can take qualifications that are recognised throughout the world.

To change the alignment of text:

Either:
Click on one of the alignment buttons on the **Home** tab before you start:

Or:
Select the text you want to align differently
And
Click on one of the alignment buttons on the formatting toolbar.

Note: **After using the centre, right align or full justification, you must remember to click the left align button to return to normal typing.**

Centring Text on a Page

You can vertically centre text on a page. This is useful for documents such as menus or advertisements.

To do this:
- Click anywhere on the page, either before or after typing the document.
- Go to the **Page Layout** tab of the **Ribbon Bar**. Click on the box at the bottom right hand corner of the **Page Setup** group to open the full menu. Go to the **Layout** tab and where it says **Vertical Alignment**, click **Centre**. Click **OK**.

Changing the Paper Size

Most office documents are produced on A4 Portrait Paper. Occasionally, however, a different size is needed, or the A4 needs to be 'Landscape' style. To change the paper size:

◆ Go to the **Page Layout** tab of the **Ribbon Bar**.
◆ Click on the **Size** button and select either A4 or say A5.
◆ Click on the **Orientation** button and select either **Portrait** or **Landscape**.

Using Print Preview

Many changes that you make to a document do not show on the screen, for instance a document centred from top to bottom. The Print Preview feature lets you see how your centred text will appear on a printed page.

◆ Click on the **Office Button**. Hover the mouse over **Print** and from the menu that appears, click **Print Preview**.
◆ To magnify an area of the page, position your mouse pointer over an area and click to magnify it.
◆ When you have finished previewing your document, click **Close Print Preview** and you will return to your normal screen.

Using Tabs

You use tabs to line up columns of information in a document. Although Word has 'preset' tabs they are not always in the right place.

There are four kinds of tab that you can set: **Left**, **Right**, **Centre** and **Decimal**. They are situated at the very left of the ruler line and only one type will show at a time. You can set as many different tabs across the ruler line as you wish.

The four kinds of tabs are shown below:

The following instructions will help you to set up and alter your own tabs:

To set tabs

◆   Click on the button on the left edge of the ruler to choose the type of tab required (left, right, centre or decimal).
◆   Click on the bottom of the ruler to position the tab. Repeat as necessary.

To alter existing tabs
Select the text.
Either drag the existing tab stops along, or drag the existing tab stops down and replace with different tab stops.

Note: When you have finished with your tabs, click on each one in turn and drag downwards.

Headers and Footers

Headers and Footers are used to display information that you want to appear on every page, for example, the title of the document or the page number. The Header is at the top of the page and the Footer at the bottom. You can choose to have a different Header and Footer for the first page of the document if necessary. Information that you insert into the Header and Footer displays in light grey on your screen if you are using **Print Layout** view (it does not show in other layouts) and can also be seen when you go into **Print** Preview.

If you require page numbering, you should set this up before you add any other text to the Header and Footer.

To add Page Numbering

Word can automatically number the pages in your document. If you add, remove or re-arrange text in your document, Word will automatically adjust the page numbers for you.

◆   Click on the **Insert** tab of the **Ribbon Bar**.
◆   Click on the **Page Number** button, click to select where you want your page numbers to appear, eg, top of page, bottom of page etc. From the menu that appears, click to select the style and positioning of numbers that you want.
◆   When you have selected how you want your page numbers to appear, the **Header and Footer Tools** tab will appear and the **Header and Footer** areas will be displayed on your page. At this point you can add any other text you want to display.
◆   Click **Close Header and Footer** to go back to your main document.
◆   If you don't want page numbering to start at 1, you can choose the number that page numbering starts at by clicking on the **Page Number** button, clicking **Format Page Numbers, Start At** and entering the number you want to start at, followed by **ok**.

To add a Header or Footer without Page Numbering.

◆ Click on the **Insert** tab on the **Ribbon Bar**.
◆ Click on the **Header** or **Footer** button and select the layout you require.
◆ The Header or Footer will now be displayed on screen, as will the **Header and Footer Tools** tab. Enter your text and when you have finished either double click elsewhere on the page or click the **Close Header and Footer** button on the **Ribbon Bar.**

You can go back to the Header or Footer at any time by double clicking in that area of the page.
To have a different Header and Footer on the first page, click the **Different First Page** button on the **Header and Footer Tools** tab.

Inserting a Page Break

If you want to start a new page at a specific place in your document, you can insert a page break. To do this you can either:

Click where you want to start a new page and then hold down **Ctrl** and press the **Enter** key.
Or
Click where you want to start a new page and click on the **Insert** tab of the **Ribbon Bar**.
Click the **Page Break** button.

Changing Margins

To change your margins for a document:

Click on the **Page Layout** tab of the **Ribbon Bar**.
Click on the **Margins** button.
Pick one of the options. Alternatively, if you want to select your own margins click on **Customise Margins**, change the **left, right, top** and **bottom** to your requirements and click **OK**.

More Advanced Features in Word

Tables

You can create a table to display columns of information in your document. As far as Word is concerned, a table consists of columns, rows and cells.

- A column is a vertical line of boxes
- A row is a horizontal line of boxes
- A cell is one box

In order to create a table:

- Click where you want your table to be.
- Go to the **Insert** tab and click on the **Table button**.
- A dialogue box will appear. Say how many rows and columns you want by hovering the mouse over the squares to highlight them. Click with the left button when the table is the required size.

In order to enter text in your table:

- Click in the cell where you want to enter text. Then type the text.
- Repeat until you have finished entering all the text.

Note: You can format text in a table as you would format any text in a document, ie, add bold, italic, underline, change font size etc.

Should you want to delete your table:

- Click anywhere in the table you want to delete. The **Table Tools** tabs will appear on the **Ribbon Bar**.
- Click on the **Layout** tab.
- Click on the **Delete** button.
- Click on **Delete Table**.

An example of a simple table:

January	February	March	April
Susan	Rosemary	Kelly	Chris
Jane	Emma	Sam	Abby

Merging Cells for Titles

You can combine two or more cells in your table to create one large cell. This is useful when you want to display a title in a cell at the top of your table.

To do this:

Position the mouse over the first cell you want to merge with other cells.
Drag the mouse until you highlight all the cells you want to merge.
Click on the **Table Tools Layout** tab.
Click **Merge Cells**.

An example

MONTHS OF THE YEAR			
January	February	March	April

Adding and Deleting Rows and Columns

To add a row:

◆ Select the row above or below where you want the new row to be. Do this by positioning your mouse to the left of the row (outside the table). Look for the mouse pointer arrow and click to select the row.
◆ Click on the **Table Tools Layout** tab.
◆ In the **Rows and Columns** group click on **Insert Above** or **Insert Below**.
◆ The new row should appear in your table.

To delete a row:

◆ Select the row to be deleted.
◆ Click on the **Table Tools Layout** tab.
◆ Click on the **Delete** button.
◆ Click **Delete Rows**.

Note: To quickly add a row at the end of a table, click in the last cell of the last row and then press the Tab key on the keyboard.

Adding or deleting a column is done in exactly the same way except:

Position the mouse over the top of the column and the pointer will change to a dark down arrow. Click to select the column.

And

Choose **Insert Left, Insert Right** or **Delete Columns** instead of rows.

Adding a Gap Above or Below Text

It can look good to spread your table out a little rather than have the lines of text very close to the lines in the table. To do this:

- ◆ Select the table. When selecting the table remember to take the mouse to the left of the table – outside – and watch for the pointer to change into an arrow. Click and drag down through the table.
- ◆ Click on the **Page Layout tab**.
- ◆ In the **Spacing** section of the **Paragraph** group, click on the up arrow next to **Before** and **After**, increasing it to what you want (usually a 6 pt gap or half line space).
- ◆ Click on **OK**.

An example:

MONTHS OF THE YEAR			
January	February	March	April

How to Use Borders and Shading

You can apply some shading or a special border to your table. To do this:

- ◆ Select the table or a range of cells.
- ◆ Click on the **Table Tools Design** tab.
- ◆ To change the border: Click on the down arrow next to the **Line Style** box (shown by a horizontal line) to select the line style. Click on the down arrow next to the **Line Weight** box to choose the thickness of the line. Click on the down arrow next to the **Borders** box to select where you want the border to go.
- ◆ To add shading: Click on the down arrow next to the **Shading** box and select the shade you want.

An example:

MONTHS OF THE YEAR			
January	February	March	April

Mail Merge

If you want to send the same letter to a number of different people, then the **Mail Merge** facility in Word is very useful. You can personalise each letter by setting up a datafile containing names, addresses etc. As long as you follow through each step carefully, then you will be able to create mailshots for a large number of people in no time at all.

1 Create a table of four columns and three rows and prepare your data file by copying the example on the next page, using suitable column headings, eg, name, address, saluation etc. Save the datafile in the **My Data Sources** folder, in **Documents**, or where you want to save it, giving it an appropriate name, eg, datafile A, and close the file.

2 Prepare your letter, putting in @ symbols where necessary. Copy the example on the next page but do not type the words after the @ symbols – these are for illustration only.

3 Click on the **Mailings** tab, followed by **Start Mail Merge** and then **Step by Step Merge Wizard.** The **Mail Merge Task Pane** will appear on the right.

4 In the **Mail Merge Task Pane**, where it says **Select document type** click on **Letters**. Click on **Next** at the bottom of the panel.

5 Where it says **Select starting document**, click on **Use the current document**. Click on **Next**.

6 Where it says **Select recipient**, click on **Use an existing list** and then click on **Browse. My Data Sources** will appear and you select your datafile, either from this or from wherever you have saved it. Click on **Open**. Check the details and if they are all right, click on **OK**. Click on **Next**.

7 Position the Insertion Point where you want the first Merge Field to go. Delete your @ symbol. Click on the bottom of the **Insert Merge Field** box on the **Mailings** tab and click on the field to be inserted. Repeat for the other fields. Click on **Next** in the **Task Pane.**

8 At this stage the merge has not taken place but you will see one of the letters is previewed. Click on the arrows on the **Mailings** tab to look at the other letters. You can go back into the data sources if you need to for amendments.

9 When you have finished, click on the **Finish and Merge** button on the **Mailings** tab, followed by **Edit Individual Documents** and **OK**. Your letters should be merged.

10 Save the merged document and print out the letters. Save the master document or text file (with the insertions still as codes, name, address etc) and close it.

Datafile

Name	Address	Salutation	Destination
Mrs J Smith	6 The Street Anytown ANYPLACE A057 6BJ	Mrs Smith	Devon
Mr R Jones	57 Long Road WITHAM Essex CM45 4JY	Mr Jones	Cornwall

Letter

29 August 20—

@
@

Dear @

Thank you for your enquiry about our holidays. We have pleasure in enclosing a copy of our brochure on holidays in@.

We hope you will decide to tour with us and look forward to hearing from you.

Yours sincerely

Mail Merge to include labels

Assuming that you have already performed your mail merge with your datafile saved, it may well be that you want to print labels to go with your merged letters. To do this:

1   Open a blank page. Select the **Mailings** tab, **Start Mail Merge** and **Labels**.

2   The **Label Options** box appears for you to choose the size of your labels. Select the size you want and click **OK**. A grid of label outlines will appear in your document. Click on **Select Recipients, Use an Existing List** and **Browse**.

3   In the dialogue box, select the datafile you want to use and click on **Open**. The **Mail Merge Recipients** box will open showing the information you keyed into your datafile. Click **OK**.

4   With the insertion point in the first box in your grid, you are ready to begin putting your data onto the labels. Click on the bottom of the **Insert Merge Field** box on the **Mailings** tab and click on each field in turn eg, Name, Address, to insert it. Don't worry if it says 'Next Record' on each label; this won't print out.

5   Once you have arranged your data fields, click on the **Update Labels** button to ensure all of your labels have the same format.

6   Click **Preview Results** and make any necessary amendments.

7   Click **Finish and Merge**, followed by **Edit Individual Documents** and **OK**. This creates a new document containing your actual labels with the names and addresses on. You are now able to make any changes you need to make before saving and printing them. Finally save the document that contains the label format. Close both documents.

Graphics

It is sometimes effective to illustrate your text with a graphic (picture). Microsoft Office software contains a number of pictures that you can use in what is called **Clip Art**. If you are connected to the internet you will have access to many more pictures, and you can also import your own photographs and use these in your work.

The basic method for importing a graphic is as follows:

◆   Choose where you want your graphic to appear.
◆   Click on the **Insert** tab and **Clip Art**. The **Clip Art Task Pane** will appear.
◆   Where it says **Search** for, type a word that describes what you are looking for, eg, flower. Click on **Go**. Click on the flower you would like and it will be inserted on your page.

To resize your graphic

Click in the graphic and handles (little squares) will appear. Point at one of the handles and the mouse pointer will become a double-headed arrow. Drag the pointer to the required size.

To move your graphic

Place the mouse pointer in the graphic and drag. This, however, will only move the graphic further up or down the page. If you want to put it in a specific place, see below.

To move a graphic into the centre of the text

From activity breaks in Wales to romantic weekends in one of
Europe's capital cities, our breaks are always good value for money.
Listed below are some of the two day European breaks we offer.

- Create the graphic in the normal way, underneath the text.
- Make sure you have the handles round the graphic and click on **Text Wrapping** on the **Picture Tools** tab.
- Click on **Tight** from the list of options.
- Drag the picture into position.

To insert a graphic at the right of the table

January	February	March	April

- Type the table. Drag the vertical lines of the table back so there is enough room for the graphic to be inserted.
- Create the graphic in the normal way, underneath the table.
- Make sure you have the handles round the graphic and click on **Text Wrapping** on the **Picture Tools** tab.
- Click on **In Front of Text.**
- Drag the picture into position.

To insert a graphic to the left of text.

 Christopher Jones handled the motor car extremely well. He
was a quick driver and went from zero to sixty in no time at all,
but he did seem to know what he was doing and I always felt
safe at his side.

- Set a hanging indent for the text and press the tab key to move across the page.
- Type the text.
- Create the graphic in the normal way, underneath the text.
- Make sure you have the handles round the graphic and click on **Text Wrapping** on the **Picture Tools** tab.
- Click on **In Front of Text**.
- Drag the picture into position.

Using Bullets and Numbering

You can separate items in a list by beginning with a bullet or number. To do this:

On the **Home** tab, click on the **Bullets** or **Numbering** buttons on the toolbar, before typing your text.

You can change the style of bullets or numbers by clicking on the ▼ arrow next to the **Bullets** and **Numbering** buttons.

Note: You can also do this after typing by highlighting the text you wish to add bullets or numbers to and then clicking on the Bullets or Numbering buttons.

Columns

You can display text in columns like those found in a newspaper. This is useful for creating documents such as newsletters and brochures. When creating columns it is best to work in the **Print Layout** view and type the text first, changing it into columns later.

Once the text is typed:

♦ Select the text to be put into columns.
♦ On the **Page Layout** tab, click on **Columns** and select the number of columns you want.

Note: Word will put in what is called a Section Break before and after the selected section. Otherwise the whole document would go into two columns.

An example:

Every one of our items is individual and produced to the highest standard in our small home-based workshop. We pay particular attention to the finish, both in terms of the mosaic itself and the board on which it is mounted.

Many of our designs are geometric and some date from Roman times. We also use

the 'Gaudi' style of modern mosaic, named after Antoni Gaudi who was an acclaimed Spanish architect in the late 19th and early 20th century. He used mosaic made out of small irregular shapes, rather like miniature crazy paving, to decorate wonderful buildings and parks in Barcelona.

It is also possible to put a picture in the columns. This is achieved by choosing **Tight** in **Text Wrapping** (**Picture Tools** tab) and then moving it into position.

PART 4
REFERENCE GUIDE

Important Symbols and General Rules

Capital letters

When a group of letters or words are in capitals it is best to use the **Caps Lock** key. Usually a light will show that it is switched on. For single capital letters, one of the shift keys should be used.

There are a number of rules for the use of capital letters at the beginning of a word:

◆ Always start a sentence with a capital letter
◆ Always use a capital for the word 'I' when talking about yourself
◆ Use a capital at the start of direct speech
◆ Use initial capitals for names of people, places and proper nouns
◆ Use initial capitals for titles of books, films etc
◆ Use capitals for days of the week and months of the year, but not for seasons.

Look at the following:

The name of the company was WILLIAM BLACKMAN ASSOCIATES.
Add FOUR eggs and FOUR teaspoons of milk to the mixture.
The latest book by Alison Stuart is called 'The Driver'.
I am going to Spain in July. I love sitting in the sun.

Hyphens and dashes

The same key is used for both functions.

The hyphen comes between two words, eg, sky-scraper, or instead of the word 'to', eg, 18-20 High Street. It does not have a space either side of it.

The dash is used if a breath or a pause is taken. It is often used instead of brackets or a comma. It always has a space on either side.

Look at the following:

The re-covering of the chairs was really necessary.
From 18-20 January we expect to be in Kings Street.
If I have to go – as is possible – I will ring you.
The show – the only one this month – was very good.

Exclamation mark

As its name suggests, this mark indicates an exclamation and it should be used very sparingly. Its general use is to inject humour or emphasis into a sentence or paragraph.

Look at the following:

What a silly girl you are! Fancy falling over in the playground.
Bravo! You have really done so very well.

Question mark

A question mark is shown at the end of a sentence which asks a question. It can also be used in business correspondence to show a query on a date or time etc.

Look at the following:

Why are you going now? Can I go to the house with you?
Can you see her? Is she in the top row or at the back?
The letter is due to arrive by ? February at the latest.

Round brackets

When using brackets in a sentence, make sure the sentence still makes sense if the brackets are removed. Generally speaking, the words in the brackets should add some extra explanation to the sentence. Do not use a capital letter for the first word in the bracket, unless for a particular reason. Similarly, a full stop is not needed at the end of the bracketed words.

Look at the following:

Entries (preferably on a postcard) to be sent to us by tomorrow.
Rachel King (the new committee member) will address the meeting.

Square brackets

These are rarely used. Their only real use is to show an addition to a direct quotation:

Look at the following:

Mr Brown said in his report: 'I am so sorry about the lack of pay rise this year, but I hope that you [the employees] will understand the situation.'

Quotation marks

These are used for quotations or direct speech. Either single or double can be used according to preference.

Try the following:

"My project for the year is 'The Rain Storm'," said Tom.
'I hope you will be able to see our new play "Rafters",' said Mary.

Apostrophes

This is the same symbol as the single quotation mark.

An apostrophe is used for two reasons:

1) To show possession.
    The cat's owner lives up the road. (the owner of the cat)
    The plural is shown in two ways:
    The ladies' shoes were made of leather. (s' apostrophe as 'ladies' ends in s)
    The children's shoes were all over the room. (apostrophe + s because the subject, 'children' does not end in s)

2) To show omission.
    An apostrophe can be used to shorten words and is placed at the point where the letters are missing, eg, don't, won't, I've, it's, you're.

Look at the following:

Susan's friend was Hilda. Hilda's mum knew Susan's mum.
Your shoes are the smartest I've seen. They're so cool.
The dog hurt its paw. It's a good thing you were there.
The children's homework is hard. They've got lots to do.

Oblique, solidus or slash

This is used in references or to show options.

Look at the following:

I have the reference to MCD/645 when I typed the letter.
I/we are hoping to show my/our pictures at the gallery.

Ampersand or &

This should only be used in company names, in accepted abbreviations, or in tables where space is at a premium.

Look at the following:

Smith & Jones, together with Brookers & Son, came today.
E & OE, if on forms means Errors and Omissions Excepted.

More General Rules

Numbers

Generally speaking, and unless given specific instructions, numbers can be expressed in either figures or words, so long as consistency is maintained within a document. In newspapers, words are usually used up to 10 and then figures above 10. This is also acceptable.

Sums of money within continuous text

Pounds and pence have a decimal point (full stop) separating them, eg, £6.50. Always take the pence figure to two decimal places and never type £ and p in one sum. If only pence are involved they can be expressed as 50p or 50 pence. If only pounds are involved there is no need to take the figures to two decimal places, eg, £12, £14.

Measurements and weights

When typing metric measurements or weights, leave one space after the figures before the unit of measurement. Abbreviations are acceptable. You do not need to add an 's' for a plural.

Examples of metric measurements and weights:
16 mm, 18 cm, 10 kg.
Feet and inches can be written in one of the two following ways:
6' x 4" (using the single and double quotation marks with no space after figures)
or
6 ft x 4 in (leaving one space after the figures)
Note: and 'x' can be used for 'by', eg, 5' x 24".

Temperature

Metric temperature is expressed as degrees Celsius (°C).

Examples of temperatures:
26 °C, 14° – a space is left after the figures if C follows the degree sign, but no space is left if it does not.

Date

Normally type the date as day, month and year with no punctuation in between:
13 September 20XX.

Twelve and twenty-four hour clock

When typing the twelve hour clock, am or pm should be inserted one space after the figures and a full stop should be placed between the hours and the minutes, eg, 9.30 am, 3.00 pm. With the twenty-four hour clock, no full stop or space is inserted in the figures and the times are followed by hrs or hours. There should always be four figures showing the hours and the minutes, eg, 0930 hrs, 1500 hrs.

Line Spacing

When using a word processing program it is possible to change the line spacing according to the kind of typewritten work you are producing. There are three main types of line spacing:

Single line spacing

Single line spacing is used for most typing.

This paragraph is typed in single line spacing. This means that each line starts immediately under the one before with only a minimum of space in between.

Double line spacing

Double line spacing is used for draft documents so that corrections can be made. It is also

used to display work more effectively. This paragraph is typed in double line spacing.

This means leaving one clear line of space between every line of typing.

One and a half line spacing

This paragraph has been typed in one and a half line spacing. This means leaving half a

line of space between each line of typing. Like double line spacing it is useful for display

purposes.

Fonts

There are many different types of font available when using a modern word processing program. The word font actually means typeface. Examples of fonts are Times New Roman, which is known as a 'serif' font (with tails or fancy bits on the letters), and Arial which is known as a 'sans serif' font (without tails). Each font comes in different sizes called 'point sizes' and Times New Roman 12 will not look the same as Arial 12 because the font types are different to begin with.

With most fonts you will see that each letter takes up a different amount of space. This is called proportional spacing, eg, 'm' takes up more space than 'i'. For touch typing practice it is best to use a fixed font such as Courier New, where each letter takes up the same amount of space. Use Courier New 12 for the drills and then each line should finish at the same place.

Examples:

This is Times New Roman with a point size of 12

This is Arial with a point size of 12

`This is Courier New with a point size of 12.`

Margins

It is usual to have 2.5 cm or 1" all round a document. Most word processing programs will set this automatically for you.

Paper Sizes

A4 Portrait Paper

210mm (8 ¼")

297mm (11 ¾")

A4 Landscape Paper

297mm (11 ¾")

210mm (8 ¼")

Paper Sizes

A5 Portrait Paper

148mm (5 7/8")

210mm (8 1/4")

A5 Landscape Paper

210mm (8 1/4")

148mm (5 7/8")

Manuscript Correction Signs

Sign	Meaning	Example
CAPS OR VC	Change to capital letters	Minutes of the Meeting ✎ (CAPS)
lc	Change to small letters	Where is the Pool? Lc
Sp CAPS	Change to spaced capitals	AGENDA ⟵ Sp Caps
/ or #	Leave a space	The books are due today.
⌒ or close up	No space between characters or words	They arrived be⌒fore lunch.
Stet or ✓	These signs in margin mean put back crossed through words with dotted line below	Her exam results were poor and she is very lazy. ✓
ʌ	Insert additional matter at point shown	weather permitting Tomorrow we shall have a picnic.
|| NP or [	Start a new paragraph at the point indicated	Thank you for your letter. [When I see you next week, shall we go out to lunch?
⌐ or run on	Do not start a new paragraph	We did very well last year. Next year should be even better.
⌀ or word crossed out	Deletions – words removed	We apologise for the serious error.
⊔⊓	Reverse order horizontally	She was pretty, slim and young.
⊐ or (↕)	Reverse order vertically	Smith P / Smith M (Smith P / Smith M)
(CEDAR)	An unfamiliar or badly written word is shown in the margin. It should not be typed in capitals	The house had a lovely cedar tree.

Abbreviations and their Correct Spellings

accom	accommodation
a/c(s)	account(s)
advert(s)	advertisement(s)
approx	approximately
appt(s)	appointment(s)
asap	as soon as possible
bn	been
bus	business
cat(s)	catalogue(s)
co(s)	company(ies)
cttee(s)	committee(s)
dr	dear
def	definitely
dept(s)	department(s)
dev	develop
exam	examination
ffly	faithfully
f/t	full-time
hr(s)	hour(s)
immed	immediately
info	information
mfr(s)	manufacturer(s)
misc	miscellaneous
mth	month
necy	necessary
org	organisation
p/t	part-time
poss	possible
prob	probably
rec'd	received
ref(s)	reference(s)
resp	responsible
sinc	sincerely
sh	shall
shd	should
temp	temporary
thro	through
w	with
wd	would
wh	which
wl	will
yr(s)	your(s) year(s)

Putting Together Sentences and Paragraphs

Almost all typing involves the use of sentences, paragraphs and headings. It is therefore important to know something about the construction of sentences and paragraphs and how to display them along with their headings.

Sentences

According to The Oxford Guide to the English Language, a sentence is 'a set of words making a single complete statement'. To put it another way, a sentence must make sense and it must have a *subject* and a *predicate*.

- The subject is the person or thing being discussed in the sentence. It is normally a noun (a name of a person or thing, eg, Sarah, John), or a pronoun (a word used instead of a noun, eg, he, she).
- The predicate says something about the subject and it must contain a verb (a doing word, eg, speaks, ran).

Example of a sentence:

Sentences can be short or long, but never make them longer than necessary. Long sentences can be used in descriptive work. Short sentences are better for giving emphasis or a sense of urgency. Try to keep just one item in each sentence otherwise the meaning becomes clouded.

Paragraphs

A paragraph is one or more sentences grouped around a central theme or subject. When that theme or subject changes, a new paragraph should begin. Every paragraph should have one sentence which describes the theme or subject for that whole paragraph.

Like sentences, paragraphs can vary greatly in length, but generally speaking they should not be too long or else the effect of the meaning is weakened.

Different kinds of paragraphs

Blocked

A blocked paragraph means that every line starts at the set left hand margin as in this example.

In common with all paragraphs an extra line of space should be left between them.

This blocked method is quick to type and neat in appearance.

Indented

This is the indented style where the first line of each paragraph begins approximately half an inch (1.25 cm) in from the left margin. These are rarely used nowadays.

Hanging

This type of paragraph is even more rare, but it does sometimes appear in examinations.

This is a hanging paragraph and, as you will see, the first line starts to the left of the rest
    of the paragraph.

Numbered and lettered paragraphs

1   This is a numbered paragraph. The number can be set 'inside' the paragraph like this.

2   This is also a numbered paragraph, but with the number left 'outside' as in this example.

a   This is a lettered paragraph and it can be used in either of the above ways, although 'outside' tends to be clearer.

(b) This is yet another lettered paragraph with the letter typed inside brackets.

Note: When typing in single line spacing, one clear line should be left between paragraphs (2 x return). The same applies to double line spacing (2 x return).

Headings

Blocked or shoulder headings

These are the most common headings in use today. They usually accompany blocked paragraphs. The heading is typed at the left margin and then at least one line of space is left before typing the text. Headings can be typed in closed capitals, spaced capitals, or initial capitals. With spaced capitals, leave one space between each letter and three spaces between each word.

Centred heading

This heading, as you will see, appears in the centre of the typing line.

Paragraph heading   With this type of heading, the heading is typed first, then three spaces are left and the text is typed on the same line. As in this example, emphasise the heading in some way, using italics, underline, bold or capital letters.

Side or marginal heading   This type of heading is often used for minutes of meetings or a Curriculum Vitae, where the headings are set down the left hand side of the page, with at least two spaces after the longest line before the text begins.

The Business Letter

The business letter is a very important form of communication. It should be:

- Well presented

- Brief and to the point

- Accurate

- Easy to read and understand.

Planning a letter

As with all forms of written communication, decide first on the purpose of your letter and what you want to achieve. Then make a list of the points to be covered.

Your letter should contain an opening paragraph which sets the scene for the rest of the letter. The main points to be covered should be sub-divided into further paragraphs. The final paragraph normally contains a summing up of the contents and any recommendations. Do not make your sentences or paragraphs too long.

Most letters are produced with what is known as the *fully blocked* layout and using *open punctuation*. This means all the typing starts at the left of the page and there is no punctuation except in the main body of the letter.

The parts of a business letter

1   The company printed heading.

2   References. Only insert a 'Your Ref' if previous correspondence from the recipient shows a reference. 'Our Ref' is usually the initials of the sender and of the typist, plus a file number if appropriate.

3   The date. All letters must be dated.

4   Any special message. 'For the Attention of', 'Confidential' etc.

5   Name and address of the person the letter is going to. Use a separate line for the postcode and put the post town in capitals. (For foreign addresses put the country in capitals.)

6   The salutation or greeting. Use a personal name if possible rather than Dear Sir/Madam.

7   The subject heading.

8   Main body of letter, subdivided into paragraphs.

9   Complimentary close. Use 'Yours faithfully' if letter starts 'Dear Sir/Madam' and 'Yours sincerely' if letter starts 'Dear Mr Bloggs'.

10 The name of the company can, if required, be shown after the complimentary close.

11 The name of the sender and his/her designation (position).

12 The enclosure mark. This indicates that something has been enclosed with the letter. Sometimes you will see 'att' for attached. This means much the same.

1   COMPANY HEADED PAPER

2   Your ref CWJ/ABD
     Our ref   PJD/PS
     @

3   2 July 20XX
     @

4   URGENT
     @

5   Mrs A Boyd
     23 Sheland Street
     CENTRETOWN
     Norfolk
     NR54 90J
     @

6   Dear Mrs Boyd
     @

7   CHRISTMAS PROMOTION
     @
     You may remember that we wrote to you in March asking for your expected requirements this year. You kindly sent us an estimated figure but asked us to contact you again later on.
     @

8   We are now preparing our Christmas programme and enclose a copy for your perusal. You will see that TEDDY BEAR FLASHING LIGHTS are a new addition to our usual range and we are sure that at £10.99 a set they will prove to be a real winner.
     @
     If you would like further information on any of the products contained in the programme, our representative will gladly call on you. Otherwise we look forward to receiving your order by post or fax by the end of July.
     @

9   Yours sincerely

10 DASERS ENTERTAINMENT LTD
     @
     @
     @
     @

11 Phillip J Dean
     SALES DIRECTOR
     @

12 enc

Note: @ = 1 clear line space

Memos

Like a letter, a memo is a form of written communication. Unlike a letter, however, it usually stays within an organisation and passes from one department to another as internal correspondence. Most companies have their own headed memo paper. An example of a memo is shown below:

MEMORANDUM

From	Alan Carter
To	Alice Smith
Date	22 November 20XX
Ref	AC/ABC

CLOSURE OF SNACK BAR

A memo has been sent to all office staff advising them of the closure of the snack bar from 6-13 December.

As soon as you receive the Order Sheets from the various personnel, you should log the requirements in your own book. Send off your order to Plank & Co by 3 December, so that there are no 'hitches'. I am enclosing a list of products I think you should be including in the order.

Thank you for all your help with these arrangements.

enc.

Points to remember when typing a memo

◆ The contents of a memo are usually much less formal than in a business letter because the people normally know each other.

◆ There is no address as there is on a business letter as the memo is usually internal.

◆ The main body of the memo should be typed in single line spacing.

◆ If an enclosure or attachment is mentioned, type 'enc' as in a business letter. Leave a few lines of space before typing this to allow for someone to initial the memo before it is sent out.

E-mails

Over the last few years e-mails have become one of the most important ways to communicate between individuals in the same organisation, or with other people all over the world. An e-mail is very simple to prepare and send, and the main benefit is that it can be sent immediately, with no trip to the post box and no stamp!

When you go 'on-line', your Internet Service Provider will give you an e-mail account and you can usually choose your own e-mail address. This is often your name followed by an @ sign and the address of your ISP. For example:

joebloggs@btconnect.com

E-mail Etiquette

Do

◆ Use a common e-mail program such as Outlook or Outlook Express if possible. These are designed to work with other Microsoft programs and will make your life easier. Most of the hints given in this section apply to these two programs.

◆ Treat your e-mail as a written piece of correspondence and make sure you use properly constructed sentences and paragraphs.

◆ Send any important accompanying documents as 'attachments' to your e-mail. With text it is best to use Microsoft Word attachments. The reason for this is that if you try to incorporate complicated text or graphics in the e-mail itself, the computer language might not convert it in the same way at the other end.

◆ Make sure you click on 'Send' to send your e-mail, and from time to time click on 'Send and Receive', so that your Inbox and Outbox are kept up to date. Respond to incoming e-mails promptly.

◆ Use good housekeeping for your e-mails just the same as for your other documents and file them in relevant folders.

◆ Check and delete the e-mails in your 'Deleted Items' and 'Sent Items' folders from time to time.

◆ Make sure you enter the **exact** e-mail address for the recipient of your e-mail. Even a dot in the wrong place means it will not arrive.

Don't

◆ Send anything confidential by e-mail. It may well be read by people who shouldn't be seeing it.

◆ Use fancy backgrounds for your e-mail. Stripes or watermarks may look effective, but when e-mails are scanned at the other end for viruses and 'spam' (unwanted junk e-mails), yours might well be thrown out and never reach its destination.

◆ Send an e-mail without a subject. If you leave out the subject there is a good chance that it won't be noticed or read.

◆ Send unnecessary e-mails, just because they are quick and simple. Too much time is wasted sending unnecessary e-mails.

◆ Send an e-mail instead of a letter for something really important. A letter has a more meaningful effect.

Reports

A report is intended to pass information from a person who has collected it to a person who has asked for this information. Reports in some shape or form are very common in business life. They can cover many subjects and they can be very simple as well as very complex.

Planning a report

Before compiling any report, certain questions should be asked:

♦ What is the purpose of the report?

♦ Who is going to read it?

♦ How will you obtain the necessary information?

♦ How will you present the report?

Once you have the answers to these questions clear in your mind you are ready to start preparing your report.

Typical structure of a report

Most reports will contain the following:

◆ The title.

◆ The introduction – stating what the report is about.

◆ The main body – where all the relevant information is set out and sub-divided into paragraphs as necessary. Make sure you proceed in a logical way, leading the reader on from one point to the next.

◆ The conclusion and any recommendations – giving definite reasons for both.

◆ Acknowledgements – if someone has helped you with your report, then it is polite to mention their name at the end. Similarly, if you have used material from books or newspapers, you should list your sources.

◆ Appendices – for any additional information.

Compiling a report step-by-step

Make sure you know the purpose of the report.

Decide what the report should aim to achieve.

Gather together all the relevant information.

Sort the information into logical order.

Prepare a first draft of the report.

Read and amend where appropriate.

Prepare a final copy of the report.

Circulate the report as necessary.

There are many different ways of presenting a report. The example on the next page shows a simple presentation.

REPORT ON VISIT BY ROBERT POWER TO PROPOSED NEW CARAVAN SITE AT BEACHY POINT, NEWTOWN, DORSET

Date of Visit: Friday 14 December 20—

I met Robin Payne on site at 0930 hours. He explained that the land available extended to 200 acres, which should be sufficient for our needs.

ACCESS

Access did not appear to be a problem. There were three access roads leading onto the site and all of these joined a main road within half a mile.

SUITABILITY OF LAND

The entire site was reasonably flat and would need little levelling. There were a number of trees, many of which would have to stay, but these should not present any problems.

PRICE

The negotiated price would seem to be a fair one. It would obviously be a huge commitment to all of us involved, which must be carefully thought about.

CONCLUSION AND RECOMMENDATIONS

My own conclusion was that the investment would be a good one. The site seemed absolutely ideal. I would recommend that everyone gives this matter immediate consideration as other parties are now interested in purchasing the site too. Please could I have your decisions by Monday 7 January 20—.